Eppy's Law

JERRY EPPY

authorHOUSE®

AuthorHouse™
1663 Liberty Drive, Suite 200
Bloomington, IN 47403
www.authorhouse.com
Phone: 1-800-839-8640

First published by AuthorHouse 11/17/2008

ISBN: 978-1-4389-1619-4 (sc)

Library of Congress Control Number: 2008909839

Printed in the United States of America
Bloomington, Indiana

This book is printed on acid-free paper.

CONTENTS

INTRODUCTION

The inspiration for this book comes from the 15th century philosopher, Francis Bacon. Even though it has been more than 30 years since Jerry Eppy read Bacon's Essays, he can still quote from them. While he does not think that he can verbalize his own thoughts well enough to be remembered or quoted, he still hopes that his comments on some of the modern world situations and problems can inspire some changes for the better in the world.

Jerry Eppy's intended audience is anyone and everyone, but he hopes that his essays will become a required reading for some philosophy, sociology, civics, or law courses. He would like to see these topics debated academically with the hope that they may influence the thinking of the younger generation.

Some of the topics involve moral or religious issues. Effort has been made to make the essays available to the "general reader" market instead of through a religious bookstore. Not only does he want to avoid preaching to the choir, he also feels that more action will come from people who are interested in reading broader topics than those found in a religious bookstore. Provoking action is his goal.

Eppy's Law

Consider "Eppy's Law": The attributes needed for getting elected are the opposite of the attributes needed for doing a good job in the office.

A good politician will tell the people what they want to hear. Now you might think that is good. Many times it would be good if he were sincere. Insincerity in telling them things contrary to his convictions is dishonesty. But a good politician must do it anyway. To do otherwise is to lose votes. The group listening to his statements may have narrow views, related to who they are, such as oil executives or conversely, truck drivers who use oil. But he often will tell the oil executives one thing while he is talking to them, and the truck drivers something opposite about oil when he is talking to them. Having an insincere person, or one who tries to please whomever he is talking to at the moment, holding an important position in government, is not good. But that is the type most likely to convince the public to vote for him.

The most obvious example of general promises to the public is taxes. Of course, everyone will vote for someone who promises to lower taxes. Sometimes though, there may be things that need more tax money. For example, maybe Social Security needs additional funds. Or maybe we need bigger prisons. Or maybe we need better street repair. Will he really cut taxes when he gets into office? If he cuts taxes when he should not, then he is a bad administrator. If he does not cut taxes, then he misled the voters. In either case, something is wrong about having a person in office who was not straight forward about taxes in his campaign.

Now I have to mention at this point that there is another important factor. In order to get elected, it is important to have friends and ask others for help. Now this means that the person who got elected owes favors to a lot of people. Many times, the people he must appoint to positions are not the best available for that job, but he must repay a favor. Again, this quality that makes a lot of friends might be the cause of the government having a lot of unqualified workers, or worse, some bad administrators.

Generally, the office that we are trying to fill in an election is either for an administrator, a legislator (lawmaker), or a judge. Of course, the judge should be an attorney. But we very often end up with a lawyer in those other positions. If the position is for administration, maybe it should be someone with experience as an administrator. Maybe we should elect people who have experience heading up a major operation, like a President or Superintendent of something. If the position is for a legislator, we should have a lawyer on the staff of the legislator to help with the wording of the legislation, but the legislator himself should be someone who knows something about the needs of the public and who understands economics. Hopefully, he would be a person who is well known by the public as a trustworthy and competent person who could be counted on to recognize the need for action and to do the right thing. Where is Davy Crockett when you need him?

Quite often, the personality that knows what to say and how to dress and where to be, is more of an expert in self-image than in government administration. But the public can only go by some very superficial views of the superficial candidate, and that may be enough of a show for the superficial image to get him elected.

Engineers are traditionally nerds and therefore could not get elected. The exception was Herbert Hoover. I really don't know how that happened. History books are usually not very complimentary to him. Maybe that is just because his public relations skills were not his strong point. Anyway, he was not reelected. He must have done something right though, because they named that dam thing after him.

Because of the size of our Country, we count on political parties to select the candidates for us. We cannot all know enough about everyone to find the candidates ourselves. We trust them to pick a good one. That is a good system, except that the political parties tend to pick candidates who can get elected, rather than ones who would do the best job in the position for which they are elected. (See the first paragraph.)

Sometimes, just the name recognition is sufficient to determine the election. I am not sure if the voter thinks that he is voting for the person who made the name famous or if he knows that it is a different person but thinks that if the original one was good (or at least didn't cause the world to end) then his relatives must also be good. Now, if you think that this is a trivial explanation for this phenomenon, let me remind you that the political parties find that it is worthwhile for them to pass out literature to people as they enter the polling place. In other words, they know that a significant number of people do not know who they will be voting for, even as they enter the polling place. Apparently, they look at the names on the ballot when they get to the polling place and make their decision at that time. It must be comforting to vote for a name you have heard before.

Often, the unions will endorse a candidate whose philosophies are in accordance with their needs. They will give that information to their members and strongly encourage them to vote for them. That is good. But when the union members get to the poles, they often find that there are more offices to be voted on than just the ones that they were prepared to vote on. They will often resort to name recognition, which quite often only means that the candidate has been in office before (or tried to be). It does not mean that they did a good job in the office. It could also mean that they campaigned hard enough that their name was remembered. It has nothing to do with capability.

There is one factor that helps keep the bad people from getting elected. We can be sure that their opposition will tell us everything bad about their opponent. I wish they could also evaluate their potential effectiveness for us.

I am not recommending that we change our voting system. I only wish that we could count on better preparation by our voters.

Miranda

If anyone does something vile enough to be arrested for it, they should expect that anything they say will be used against them. If they are not smart enough to know this, then maybe they need a guardian assigned to them for their own protection and to protect them from harming others.

On the other hand, if they are not involved in the criminal activity, then what would we need to warn them about saying?

Now don't confuse this with asking for an attorney. I would want someone present, not necessarily an attorney, to be a witness in case some overly aggressive interrogator threatened me or physically abused me. If I cannot readily get a friend or reputable professional of some other type, such as clergy, then an attorney will do.

Obviously, Miranda is a bureaucratic obstruction. It is probably most often omitted when a chase or struggle occurs or when the arresting officer is trying to hurry a suspect out of an area. But it really doesn't matter where or when. The point is that it is an obstruction and an annoyance at a time when the arresting officer needs to be paying attention to other matters. It is only required because some lawyers needed to make smoke to get some client off.

It is a law that is inconsistent with other legal practices. If I break a law that is obscure or not commonly known (by the general public, or by me), my failure to know the law cannot be used as an excuse. I will be prosecuted just the same. So, why would a criminal's failure to know that anything he says can be used against him be a reasonable defense?

Defense lawyers often use real or alleged problems with the Miranda statement to get a criminal set free. It is just one more obstacle to protecting you and me from criminals.

Since there is no need for Miranda, and there are terrible consequences associated with a less than perfect application at the time of arrest, we must make changes in the law and eliminate the Miranda requirement.

TRIBAL WARS

Tradition can be a wonderful thing. Look at the richness that comes from English literature or the comfort and encouragement that comes with the Catholic traditions. Then look at the role of tradition in the longstanding tribal wars. Why do some cultures incubate the passions and attitudes that promulgate tribal wars and other long-term intercultural struggles? To be sure, everyone thinks that their own way of life – culture, religion, customs – are more proper than foreign (to them) cultures. But peaceful coexistence would seem more attractive than killing and being killed.

The struggles can be for control of a country, either politically or economically. We have African nations where one of the tribes takes control of the food and medical supplies sent in by charitable nations. They basically steal the supplies for their own tribe and starve the others. Some African tribes seem to be trying to eradicate other tribes by killing them. Maybe this is a large scale "survival of the fittest", but humans are supposed to be above that method.

The Irish have been fighting amongst themselves for centuries. Which side you are on is determined by your religion. But I don't think they are fighting about religion. I am sure it started that way several centuries ago, but I think that now it is motivated more by politics or getting even for whatever the other side did. That "getting even" syndrome must be what kept the Hatfields and McCoys at each other's throats for several generations. How could they ever "even up"? Each side would always think that the other side over-did it. A disaster is always going to make a bigger impression on the one receiving the blow than the one delivering the shot. Isn't anyone smart enough to step back and look at the big picture? No one could ever win or even come out even.

Now that brings us to the Palestinians and the Jews. I think it all started before David and Goliath. Remember, not only was Goliath from Gath (Gaza maybe?), but he was a Philistine. The morphosis of a name from Philistine to Palestine over a 3000 year period is easy to see. Maybe this is a 3000 year old tribal war. What isn't easy to see is how these "tribes" can be so caught up in the latest "situation" that they do not see the overall picture. The violence is not going to end until they are able to stop trying to even up.

Certainly, people need a place to live. And sure, it would be nice to have control over where they live. And, I know it would be great if they could live at the location of certain traditional or "Holy" places. But after more than fifty years of trying to regain control of their traditional ground, it seems that further loss of lives might not be a price worth paying for that specific land. Maybe it is time (or way past time) to settle for a different place to live or a shared occupation and control of that land.

Let's look at the pros and cons of settling. First the cons:

1. Favored Holy Sites may lie outside the area of their direct government control. However, there may be a way to negotiate for ownership and control of these sites by an acceptable third party.

2. Embarrassment over failure to achieve a goal – especially of having to give in to a traditional arch-enemy.

3. Having to be reminded of the loss every time a trip is made into the Israel or Palestine territory. This will only be important for one or two generations – maybe about 30 years.

Now, the pros:

1. No loss of lives caused by an enemy who feels the need to "even up".

2. No need to have some of the people setting around thinking of ways to kill people.

3. Having a place to live and call home.

4. Having the opportunity to establish a government that will develop an infrastructure for quality of life, safety, and cultural and economic advancement.

5. Having a better chance for the children to be educated and grow up in a peaceful environment with stability and opportunity.

6. The pride of having a country.

Now that brings the question: Why can't the leaders of these countries see this obvious benefit? The answer is that they cannot go against the tradition because they would offend all those around them who are following the "tribal custom" of getting even with the "enemy". They would be considered a weakling or a traitor. It will take a hero to see the benefits and sell the idea to his fellow tribesmen.

ENGLISH

Recently, a tavern owner posted a sign that said: "For service, speak English". A governmental agency picked up on it.

First of all, let me admit that it is in poor taste. However, prosecution and penalties would be ridiculous. The owner is known for his sense of humor and has posted other signs with "tongue in cheek". If the government can censor this, then it should also shut down all the comedy clubs, close down the comedy channel, ban Saturday Night Live, including all reruns, and certainly ban all reruns of the Andy Griffith Show. The Friar's Club, because of their "Roasts" should be outlawed.

It has been said that it is offensive to those of another mother tongue. If the author wanted to insult them, he could have been more direct. No, this simply states a reality of life: If you cannot communicate, you are in danger of not getting what you want. How hard is it to learn to say "Give me a beer" in English? I am sure that what he meant was that nearly everyone in that area speaks English, and no business in the area has employees who can speak every language in the world. And, while Spanish is probably the one in question (actually, I am not so sure of that), the fact remains that there are very few in that area who can speak Spanish, and probably no one working in his place can speak it. There would be no way that the government could make a rule that all businesses must have someone working for them that can speak every language in the world. Therefore, for service, they better be able to speak English!

Actually, in Florida you cannot get a teaching certificate unless you can speak Spanish. There is no conflict here. The situation is very different. In many areas of Florida, Spanish is a language spoken by a significant portion of the population, at least as a second language. It is, in many cases, the language spoken at home, and may be the only language in which the older generation is fluent. While it makes a lot of sense to teach in English, it may be very helpful in communicating with the parents or guardians if Spanish is understood and spoken by the teachers and school administrators. (It also helps if the teacher can understand what students are talking about when they think the teacher cannot understand.)

I am not against knowing Spanish as a second language, but when in Rome …

If the incident or incidents that provoked the sign were related to a visitor in the area, I believe that the people would have been helpful to them, and friendly. But I suspect that there may be people living in the area, possibly in small communities, that are keeping largely to themselves and continuing with their cultural and language customs from their former home areas. While it is their right to do so, it will present problems for them. It will limit the jobs available to them because most jobs require communication. I am not saying that they are wrong to keep apart, I am only saying that it presents a problem for both them and the others who must interact with them. While a businessman would be wise to try to reach all potential customers, it is impractical to expect him to learn all potential languages. Even though you may say that Spanish is realistically the only second language needed, that may not have been so obvious back when the business owner was in school. When I was a child, many of the older people in my area spoke German, but most of them also learned English. There are many areas where everyone speaks only English. It would be wrong to require all business people to learn, for example, Spanish. Suppose that after they learned Spanish they moved to my old neighborhood. Would we then make them learn German? If someone chooses to live in an area, he should be willing to learn to speak the language used in that area, not expect the people already living in that area to learn the newcomer's language.

The owner was asked what he would do if a deaf person entered his store. His reply was that he would hold up a bottle of beer. He said that if he wanted something to eat, he would take him to the kitchen and let him point. He said that he would serve anyone who came into his tavern. Of course, it would be easier on both parties if he could speak English.

Someone has suggested that the tavern owner hire a lawyer, who speaks a foreign language, to represent him if he is taken to court. He suggested German, since that was the heritage of many of the people in his area. I wonder how that would turn out. Would he fail because of the difficulty of getting his points across, or would he win because the Commission would see the point?

PRISON SHORTAGE

Recently, there has been talk of letting prisoners out early and only locking up the violent criminals because of a shortage of prison space. That's scary.

There are two situations that need to be considered. First, is synergism in reverse. If lazy or immoral persons sense that there are no serious bad consequences of their misbehaving, they will do whatever they think will be to their advantage regardless of how it affects others. This can be drunken driving, stealing, failing to pay alimony or other debts, selling or using drugs, or menacing others. The threat of a couple of years behind bars can be stifling. If the justice system is a joke, then the joke will be on the public (you and me).

The other consideration is the economics of it all. We need a study to determine the cost of more prisons versus the cost of crime. The costs of dealing with crime can be very high. Car insurance premiums have to cover the costs of drunk driving and other driving abuses. Homeowner insurance premiums cover arson, robbery, etc. The court system is overburdened with criminal cases now, but it will be worse and cost more if more criminal acts are committed? We need far too many police and the associated criminal justice system accessories. The cost of private security guards in business drives up the price of purchased goods. It would be nice if the police, courts and prosecutors only had to deal with each criminal only once or twice.

But costs aside, we should all want to feel safer. The only way to do that is to get the criminals off the street.

A report by the Bureau of Justice Statistics showed that the 272,111 offenders discharged in 1994 from the prisons in 15 states had accumulated 4.1 million arrest charges before their most recent imprisonment. That comes out to 15 per prisoner. We could have prevented 12 crimes for each offender if we had kept them in jail permanently after the third offense. I strongly expect that there were ten times that many crimes that they committed but they were not caught at. After all, it is pretty hard to catch and prosecute people. Of course, you already are anticipating the next statement. Within the next three years, they accumulated another 744,000 charges. That is another 2.7 per offender.

We should build more prisons than we need, even if we have to mothball them. The threat would surely be worth it. We could save some money by making some of them less secure, for use with the less violent ones.

We could even make some of them have an internal productivity, either for internal use or to raise support money. Making the prisoners work would increase the dread of going to prison and also get them used to working so that they will find it easier to adjust to a normal life when they are released.

Talk to your local politicians and state congressmen about your desire for more prisons. Don't just sit back and shake your head. Get aggressive about your feelings.

CELEBRITY

A person who is very good at something, such a music or baseball, may need and deserve special treatment. Maybe they may need time to practice their skill, such as playing a piano or shooting a basketball. Or maybe, when they are about to perform, they may need crowd control to allow them (easy) access to the stage area or baseball locker room. Or maybe they need isolation at that time to allow them to concentrate on their upcoming performance. If they are out of their home area, on tour, they may need assistance or kindness, just as any traveler would.

But this thing about "celebrity" is way over done. We treat people who are known for something as though they know everything, and that there is something special about them above and beyond their specialty. People flock to see them as they come and go. People collect things that are associated with them. The media reports their every move.

If anything, the media shows that they are like the rest of us in that they have the same inclinations, the same weaknesses, and in most cases the same unglamorous appearances when they are not made up for the public showing. There is so much depraved activity reported: drugs, drinking, infidelity, living together, and whatever, that it often appears that they are actually worse than the average person. I don't think that they are really any worse, only that they have more opportunity to partake of the evils that are all around. They have the time and money to afford them, and their affluence makes them a juicy target for the opportunists to take advantage of them. Of course, a larger percentage of their evils are made public than for the rest of us, because of their coverage by the press. That may be offset a little by the ability their money provides to buy off prosecution and maybe even buy off bad publicity.

I am a little less in awe of them than most. For example, when I was a child, Ewell (The Whip) Blackwell was an exceptionally good pitcher for the Cincinnati Reds, and Hank Sauer was an outfielder for them. My brother provided me with a baseball signed by both of them. I kept the ball until the ball that we played with at the park lost it's cover. I then brought out my signature ball and we used it for many days until it also lost it's cover.

Now, I have to admit that I would enjoy talking to any of the Presidents of the United States, or any astronaut, for example. But since I do not want to impose upon their time, or bore them to death, I will limit my curiosity to reading about their experiences. Just to prove that I practice what I preach, I once rode ten floors in an elevator with just Neil Armstrong and myself, and neither of us said a word.

Now, what is the appropriate relationship between "stars" or celebrities and the "fans"? Well, from the fans side, we should show respect and friendliness, and be willing to provide for the performer's needs, especially when they are traveling. That includes not imposing ourselves onto them.

But, most importantly, from the celebrity side, since there are many people who watch and admire them, the celebrities must act as models of proper behavior. Whether they like it or not, their conduct affects the conduct of many others. They must lead others with a conduct that is appropriate and moral. And, they must live to that standard both on and off the "stage". With the celebrity status comes responsibility!

If it is wrong for a person to use drugs or drink excessively, then it is far more wrong to lead others to use drugs or drink excessively. Those of us who have special talents have a responsibility to use them in a proper manor. Wouldn't it be wonderful if performers and leaders always threw some positive message into each performance, while they had the attention of many others? Oh well, I guess we just have to settle for hoping they don't do too much ugly activity while the media is watching.

EVOLUTION
THE BIG PICTURE

A big discussion these days is about whether the world was created in "seven days" as a literal interpretation of the Bible or whether it evolved from the "Big Bang" over billions of years.

Sometimes, it looks like the "Creation" people are the religious people and the "Evolution People" are the atheistic. This is because Creationism requires a divine intervention at each stage or day. But if you look at what would be required for an evolution from the Big Bang to humans, - it would require a subtle, yet brilliant plan to set it all up with one action and depend upon evolution to develop the result. Doing it all at once would require an even more brilliant intellect, or divinity, than step by step. Of course, it could be a combination of both, but lets look at the basic evolution process.

It starts with a tremendous concentration of energy, which begins to expand and coagulate into matter by the laws of nature regarding the conversion of mass and energy. One of these laws was discovered by Einstein:

$E=mc^2$. As the basic types of matter form, such as quarks and neutrinos and other particles, they combine to form protons and neutrons and others, which then combine to form atoms. Atoms are pulled together by gravity to form stars, planets, and galaxies.

Scientists today believe that there are only a few basic forces in the universe, and that these forces have formed the world as we see it. The forces are the "Strong Force" which causes the quarks to combine to form protons and neutrons and a few other particles, the "Weak Force" which holds the protons and neutrons together in the nucleus of atoms, the "Electromagnetic Forces" which at the level of the atom cause elements to combine to produce compounds, while at the larger levels cause energy fields, and lastly, "Gravity".

But as simple as these forces may be, the combinations that they can create are boundless. Take for example the combinations of atoms. We find on earth atoms with up to 92 protons and various numbers of neutrons (the elements). The number of protons determines which element it is, such as oxygen or carbon or sodium. Because of the electrons associated with the atom, which is related to the number of protons in the atom, the electromagnetic forces permit certain combinations with other atoms and combinations of atoms. These combinations are boundless. Materials are produced with a very wide range of properties. All of the effects of chemistry are controlled by the variations of combinations permitted by the application of these basic forces.

Not every atom will combine with every other atom. The forces only allow certain combinations, even though there are very many combinations that exist. In cases where the conditions are right, the atoms combine to form chains and things start to get pretty complicated. But even there, they follow the basic rules of nature and use only the basic forces. This is where the really far seeing parts of the plan appear.

There are a certain few combinations (molecules) of the most common atoms (elements) that are easily formed and are therefore very abundant on our planet. These are known as amino acids. A certain four of these amino acids will combine very easily with each other and, to a large extent, only with each other. The result is not just a chain, but because they can combine with three of these amino molecules at the same time, a double chain (the famous double helix). This is certainly a very strange development to occur from the few basic forces of nature. But wait! Somehow, this double strand has a tendency to split into two strands and each strand recombines with other molecules of the amino acids and the double strand replicates (makes a second copy of) itself. In other words, it grows. Imagine this just happening without being part of a master plan!

Think about it. First combining in a certain way – being composed of the amino acids. Then splitting, but retaining its strand structure. Then recombining with only the right amino acids in only the right order to replicate itself and thereby grow and at the same time retain a specific identity. That's pretty much a long shot to just happen without a plan.

But then things get even stranger. These things that grow, could just get bigger and bigger and just become big blobs. But instead, they develop a mechanism that derives energy from chemicals that they come in contact with and they use the energy to draw in and activate more of the chemical "fuel". They even evolve to where the fuel drives several different sections of the growing thing, each of which contributes to the fueling operation. We call these sections organs. We now have living things.

Keep in mind that all this is triggered and controlled by a few basic laws of physics (nature). The plan is straight forward, but the results are absolutely mind-boggling. For these results to come out of a plan certainly requires an astounding intellect.

And yet the most unlikely parts of the evolutionary process are still to be told. Consider this: For some of these organisms to reproduce, they cannot just break off a piece and have it grow as another self-contained fuel user (living thing). It can only reproduce by exposing a specially produced seed to a specially produced seed from another organism very nearly like itself except that this organism is of the other of two "sex" conditions. What? That is an absurd twist. Although there are many different kinds of these fuel-burning organisms, most of them, at least the larger ones, require this seeding and fertilization to reproduce. For something that strange to be common to so many different types of living things, suggests that they all evolved from the same ancient source. It also suggests a brilliant plan.

Now these seeds are not always spewed out en masse so that there is a good chance that they will be casually fertilized. No, in many cases they require a "male" organism to recognize another of his species as the object of his desires. This means that the "brain" or "instinct" of each different species has to have the recognition/urge component preprogrammed specifically for that species. Otherwise, we would have spiders trying to mate with cockroaches, etc. Sorry, I cannot explain how this fits into the "Four Basic Forces" theory, but I'll bet it does.

While I understand that God can do anything He wants, and maybe He stepped in at several points and initiated the next stage, I can't help thinking that He went to a lot of trouble to make it look like we evolved.

If He made it look like we evolved, maybe we better believe that we evolved. But that doesn't prove that He didn't step in at several points and initiate the next step. This essay does not conclude whether the Creationists are right or not, but only helps to understand the evolutionary process. Charles Darwin's treatise only covered a small part of the process.

EVOLUTION
THE DARWIN LEVEL

Evolution is a strange thing. It is clear that living things have been around for many millions of years, and clearly through the years there has been a continual increase in the complexity and diversity of life. But why do we not find a continuum of stages of development for most of the existing species. Not only would we expect to find fossil records (maybe we just don't have enough finds), but we would also expect to see living examples of many stages of development for each species. Why are there not intermediate stages present from the last link between, for example, the chimpanzee and the human? The argument that the survival of the fittest caused each successive improvement to totally replace the previous stage does not seem valid because the natural selection process would require nearly perfectly universal mixing to be universally valid. It also would seem that survival of the chimpanzee would have been preempted by the survival phenomenon. That is, if the chimp's line were inferior to the corresponding elements of the human line, why did it survive?

This does not mean that evolution did not occur. It probably means that the changes were not so gradual. Somehow, a minor change in the DNA must have caused a major change in the structure or in the organs or in the skin covering or something. Suddenly, we have the first goat or pig or chimpanzee. Or maybe, we just have a different type of goat or pig or whatever. We do have evidence that things do evolve gradually to taller or stronger or faster specimens. We do not, however, seem to have evidence of gradual intermediate stages leading back to common ancestors of most diverse species.

Although the evolutionary process must have included many fairly large jumps in producing some of the offspring branches, the newly evolved being cannot be too dissimilar to the being from which it came because it must be able (and inclined) to mate with something to produce offspring. It is generally very limited as to what cross mating is possible, let alone natural among animals. It is not necessary that the mate have the same new DNA characteristics, only that the new DNA characteristics are passed on to the offspring. But, again, if the changes must be gradual, where are the intermediate stages in the fossil records?

That brings up one of the reasons for believing in a supreme being (God). Even if the evolution of the DNA can be shown to progress from the amoeba to the human by simply gradually adding a few chemical links, that alone would indicate brilliancy in setting such a system in motion. But consider that in order to bring about the continuation of the process, each type of creature must mate with another of it's kind, and only of it's kind. It is beyond comprehension that such a process has been passed down from generation to generation. There has to be passed in the DNA, a tendency to want to mate, and the ability to recognize the suitable partner. This recognition has to be reset in the genes for each change. Keep in mind that bugs and animals do not have access to mirrors for them to learn what their partner should look like. What a wonderful intellect it must have been to create such a system that would evolve from an amoeba to a variety of animals and bugs based on such a system of mating.

Tasers

Tasers are one of the best things that ever happened to the police department. They can get an unruly person under control with an extremely low injury/death rate. For almost any given type of incident, the resulting safety situation is much better if a taser is used than if some other means is used to get control. Once the taser disables a person, the violence is usually over. Without it, there is often a violent struggle, or worse, the unruly person may get away and be free to cause more trouble.

Some activists have complained about tasers. A few people have died after having a taser used on them. Typically, the coroner finds that the death was due to some other cause, such as a drug overdose or something, but even if there are a few deaths caused by the taser, the overall number of deaths is less than if certain other means are used. Some activists are so concerned about their freedom to do anything they want to do, that they don't see the need for our freedom from abuse by the criminal element. Tasers help to keep those criminals under control.

The above comments are about the safety of the unruly persons. It is also very important to recognize the fact that the police personnel have a much lower injury rate when tasers are used. Their safety is at least as important as some criminal's safety.

One police officer told me the following story:

One day, he chased a car in which a man reportedly had a gun. He stopped the car and asked the man to get out. Several police officers were around the man and they had their guns trained on him. Now there had been much publicity about some accusations that had been made about police prejudice in three situations where men of his ethnic background had died during police actions. Because of the accusations, and the accompanying publicity, the man may have assumed that the police would not shoot him.

In any case, the man was told to put his hands up. Instead, he thrust them into his pockets. Then the police told him to take his hands slowly out of his pockets and put them over his head. After stalling around for a while, he jerked his hands rapidly out of his pockets and, at the same time, gave a provocative gesture. He obviously was daring the police to shoot him. Personally, I would have expected the police to shoot him, but not because of ethnic prejudice.

Then, since the police hadn't reacted violently, he proceeded to twist and dance around. He even turned a somersault. At this point, the officer said to the other officers "Does anyone have a taser?" As soon as one of the police officers produced a taser, the man knelt down and put his hands behind his back in position to be handcuffed. The crisis was over. No one was injured during the arrest, although I understand that there had been some violence leading up to the chase.

The point of all this is that we want the police to have tasers at their disposal for three reasons:

1. We want to have fewer permanent injuries or deaths caused by police action.

2. We want to have fewer injuries or deaths among police.

3. We want fewer criminals to escape during police actions.

On the other hand, I certainly do not want tasers to be available outside the police department. I do not want anyone to have the power to get me under control, except for my protection. We need to make it unlawful to possess a taser outside of law enforcement agencies.

ABORTION

You will have to read some other essay to help you understand why, but the younger half of the population today is much more self centered than we were years ago. Perhaps the greatest example of this is the more than one million abortions each year in the USA alone. I expect that each of these terminations of life has a pretty large element of selfishness by one or both of the parents (and in some cases, the grandparents).

Many people look at something like abortion as the lesser of evils. They say that an unwanted child is better off not born. That is a pretty one-sided point of view. I wonder what the aborted one would say about that. We can study that by asking all orphans who were given up voluntarily as an alternative to abortion. They are survivors of the "unwanted" situation. How many of them wish they had never been born?

I actually know of a survivor of an abortion. The young lady, about college age when I heard her speak, was partially disfigured and had some physical problems as a result of the abortion process, but she survived it. She was a cheerful and positive thinking adult who traveled about and spoke for the Right-to-Life group against abortions. It was a very moving experience for me to see and hear her.

There are those who say that an abortion only involves tissue and that it is not yet human. I guess we could carry that further and say that a newborn doesn't have all their faculties yet and since they wouldn't remember that part of life, life so far has no meaning. Therefore, they can be aborted too. In fact, up till about six years of age, the age of reason, a person might not yet be fully developed, - we can kill them off too.

The reality is, any fertilized human seed is on the road to becoming an adult human being. To stop that process is to determine who lives and who does not.

I cannot imagine that any human being should be allowed to make that decision for any other human being. Moreover, someone who would be embarrassed or inconvenienced by the presence of the child would not be inclined to have the child's best interest as there only concern. Certainly, they should not make the decision.

When is a human being's soul created? It would seem reasonable that it would be there when life begins. But in any case, if we are not sure that it is not already there, we should not take matters into our own hands and terminate the life.

Teenage

Today, most people can expect to live eighty years or more. The teenage years are from 13 to 20, seven years. That is less than 10 % of a life. But those years, high school and the start of college (maybe), are extremely important for determining a person's value and happiness for the rest of life: another 60 years, or about 75 % of life expectancy.

There can be no doubt that a good set of morals, learned and practiced in the teenage years and carried for the rest of life, will make the overall life experience more enjoyable and more valuable. Most people over 35 know the truth of that statement. I hope that we can give teenagers that wisdom.

The inclinations of young people are strong. They want to experience things for themselves. They at least want to follow certain paths either to achieve ultimate gratification or at least get to the point where they have the option of going all the way or saying "no". Sometimes the situation is presented that leads them on into irreversible conditions. Obviously, in sexual situations, this could be pregnancy, or some incurable disease. But it could also mean injury in a thrill-seeking situation, or when a boy is trying to appear "macho". It could mean prison or at least a court record in many situations. Lying or taking advantage of someone will usually ruin a person's reputation and affect future earning power, at least in his/her local community. The list of dangers is endless. The choices made in this short time can cause some real unhappiness for the following 75 % of life.

It is so easy to fall for the false promises of peer pressure, sex drives, and other temptations. For example, smoking usually starts by wanting to "fit in". That is about the ultimate in false promises. Usually, the direct opposite is true. If a person can think for them self, and has the courage to "just say no", they will usually get more respect. The person(s) whose offer (and pressure) is rejected will probably try to ridicule the one who refuses, and that friendship (?) will end, but others who see or hear about it will be positively impressed. Furthermore, what kind of friend will try to lead you to a life where you smell bad, have a habit that is obnoxious to most people, costs lots of money, very often leads to a very miserable death, and causes great frustration when you finally recognize the situation and try to quit?

Teenagers usually are unable to handle all the situations by themselves. Parents can help in many ways. One parent can be at home after school to see what goes on and who the kids are hanging out with. They can provide wholesome activities to fill in leisure time. Sports, clubs, and other supervised activities are important. Service organizations are especially important because they help people understand that others have needs and some people have very special and important needs that they are incapable of providing for themselves.

For the parents to claim that they haven't time because they both must work is a cop out. Most families where both parents work are paying for a far more elegant house with far more elegant furniture than is needed. If they understood what that ego satisfying extravagance is costing them in the development of their children, they would not even consider letting it happen.

Another way parents need to support their children is by being involved in the schooling. They need to show interest in what the kids are learning and how well they are doing in school. Children pick up on this attitude and are accordingly motivated. This interest is not only reflected in academics, but also in their behavior.

Choice of schools may help. While most schools provide adequate educational material, there are other factors that may make some schools better than others. Private schools are more expensive. While they are recommended, they are not essential. But if the public school is chosen, parents must be aware that they must be more vigilant. The parents of the private school children have made a deliberate choice and also have put up some money. That may mean that they are more involved in the education process than those who have not made specific choices and invested money in the schooling process. This may mean that some of the public school children are less well supervised by their parents than the private school children, and therefore, there is more likelihood that these children may be a negative influence on the other children. Also, there is a tendency for private schools to have more disciplinary control over the students while they are in the school environment. In any case, parents need to be involved in the teenager's schooling and in their after school activities. Schools are for learning and not for babysitting.

PALESTINE

I recently read the autobiography of Gerhard Neumann, the former head of General Electric's aircraft engine operation. He described how, in the late 1940's, he was going through the Palestine/Israel area on a bus. The bus was fired upon by Palestinians who were hiding on a hill along the route. That was over 50 years ago. They are still fighting.

A fellow wrote an article about "Road Rage". He said that the best thing to do is to let it go when someone does something annoying. He said that we should not do anything to make the situation worse. We should not try to pass the offender or tailgate the offender and especially, do not make any gestures at the offender. His point was that nothing we can do will make the situation better, but we can make it a lot worse by trying to get even. I guess there must be some parallel to the old saying "It doesn't matter whether the rock hits the glass or the glass hits the rock, it's too bad for the glass." In other words, there is nothing you can do to make the situation better, but anything you do will probably make the situation worse. And there is no use in getting yourself or some innocent bystander hurt or killed when no good can come of it.

Now, if you could apply this "road rage" principle to the Israeli – Palestinian situation, maybe things could calm down enough that they could work out a plan to make things go on in a normal, peaceful way. Then both parties could live happily ever after. Well maybe not that good, but at least it would be better than having their culture fester in hate and deprive themselves of all the advantages of a peaceful life.

There is one more saying that may have a parallel in Palestine or Israel. We are taught in driving school to drive defensively and look out for others who may be making a mistake. It is better to give way to a person even if we have the right-of-way than to be "dead right".

I don't know who hurt whom first, or who has hurt whom most. But I can see that everyone involved is suffering and will continue to suffer until they quit trying to get even. How can we get this across to them?

ADAM AND EVE

We all think that we are smart. Each of us thinks that his/her opinion is important. Even in moral decisions, we tend to make exceptions to what is known to be "right or wrong" in order to suit our particular convenience or wants. And we mentally "justify it".

This is not a new phenomenon. Whether you consider the Bible "inspired" or not, the fact remains that it contains a story that has been passed down for about 4000 years about a man and a woman (Adam and Eve) who knew that there was something that they should not do, but they did it anyway. The woman was tempted by something that she wanted, higher status (to be like God), or self-satisfaction (knowledge of good and evil). The man was tempted by peer pressure (Eve did it), and also by the same things that tempted the woman. Both tried to justify it. We all have that tendency.

This has not worked well for mankind in the past. Try thinking of a war that was not undertaken for some need or want of one party that is trivial compared to the loss of lives, even just the lives on the instigator's side. Yet they had a reason for their actions. It may not have been in line with what a neutral party would have judged as "right", but the instigator justified it in their own mind. I'll bet the Islamic countries wondered how the Christian people could kill people (Muslims) just for the right to control a certain location. In the same way, I wonder how the Islamic terrorists can kill people just because they are "infidels". (Although they may also recognize God, just in a different way.) They all justify their actions in their own mind. Each year, more that one million living beings are deprived of their lives by a parent who would find caring for a baby to be inconvenient. They find a way to justify it in their minds.

Think back to that story about the man and woman. If there were a powerful spiritual being, who had been disobeyed, doesn't it seem logical that he would create a situation where that newly acquired knowledge of good and evil would actually be a problem for the people involved. Isn't it likely that He would "let the punishment fit the crime"? He did send them into a different world that clearly included some punishment for them. And since esteem (to be like God) was involved, wouldn't it be appropriate for them to have to need the help of some higher authority, like maybe a government, or a Church, or an elder, or maybe even a Pope. Even with our knowledge of good and evil, we seem to need a somewhat detached rule making body. History has shown that individuals cannot live in communities without having some authority to control them. This is because individuals tend to make decisions that are convenient for themselves, and are not altruistic or consistent with a moral standard. People generally know what is right when it does not affect them personally, but need a higher authority to interpret the rules when the correct moral action would be hard on them.

If there is that powerful spiritual being, is he judging us by how we accept authority, or is he just punishing us by making us live this way?

DRUG PROHIBITION

There is no doubt that much of the crime in the big cities is related to the drug market. Catching drug dealers is only part of it. Gangs or syndicates are always at war over territories. They play for keeps. Anyone who is willing to ruin another person's life by selling them drugs, probably wouldn't think twice about killing a competitor, especially if he knows that the competitor would kill him if he got the chance. Add the "gang" syndrome to this and the killer would be treated as, and feel like, a hero. Of course, to get the total crime picture, we need to add in the crimes and stupid acts performed by the users while they are under the influence of the drugs, and also the crimes they commit in order to get money to pay for the drugs after they become addicted.

It has been suggested that we make it legal to sell drugs. The theory is that this would eliminate the need for the criminal element since drugs would be available on the open market. It would take the income away from the criminal element and cause them to become engaged in a more worthwhile way of life. This also assumes that we already have the full potential market being served by the present system, and no additional users would emerge if drugs were more easily available. The proof cited is the "Prohibition" of alcohol in the 1920's and the subsequent repeal.

There is a difference between alcohol and drugs. Alcohol is only addictive to a small percentage of the population. Now don't get me wrong. Drunkenness is really bad. People do stupid things while they are drunk. They do things that are harmful to themselves and also to others. The death, and permanent injury, statistics from drunken driving are staggering. (That was not a pun.) The unfortunate victims of these accidents are not always the drunken person, either. The number of bar fights, some of which result in permanent injury, are enough to keep the police and Emergency Rooms busy, which is costing us tax dollars and insurance dollars. The number of divorces (and therefore children with only one parent) resulting from drunken actions, both in the home environment (spouse or child abuse) and away from home (fooling around) is helping to ruin our society.

But those terrible consequences do not compare with the drug problem. The difference is that only a small percentage will become addicted to alcohol. In both cases, use usually starts with either curiosity or peer pressure. The peer pressure may be subtle, like wanting to do something just so others will not look down on you. But the drug addiction will grab most people before they realize it. While the drinking problem will not be a constant problem to most people, and therefore will not ruin their lives by itself, but only through their occasional misconduct, the drug problem will consume most users completely, and totally ruin their lives. The addiction itself is enough to destroy all normal family interaction, and will usually end tragically. It will probably also affect them and others by their actions, in the same way as alcohol abuse (as described above). Most people would not even try drugs if they knew how terrible their life will be if they become addicted, and how easily addiction can slip up on them. But each of us has a way of becoming blind to the truth when we want to do something. All too frequently the drug opportunity comes at a young age when the facts are not known or understood. For that reason, giving or selling drugs to a minor should be treated as severely as having sex with a minor.

No, legalizing drugs is not the answer. There are three things that we need in order to control the drug problem:

1. Enough prisons to lock up anyone involved in the drug supply, and of course the law enforcement operatives at all levels to do the job.

2. Laws against drug users, in addition to the laws against the drug suppliers, that are severe enough to be a deterrent.

3. Education, especially of the young people. We must make it known at all ages that it is not just a game, but is a matter of life or death, or at the very least, a miserable life. We must also emphasize that it is not something you can try out and then stop using. It sneaks up on you and holds you in it's miserable grasp.

We must take a proactive role in the control of drugs. The problem will not go away by itself. It is not only an individual's problem. It is a problem for all of society because of the crime committed by the suppliers, crime committed by the users while using the drugs, crime committed by the users in getting money to satisfy their addiction, and the destruction of families resulting from a family member using drugs.

Evidence

The purpose of the Fourth Amendment was to protect citizens from the government's use of power to invade their privacy and to seize their possessions. This assumed that there was no unlawful activity. It allowed search and seizure if there was reason to suspect unlawful activity. It did require that a specific person attest to the reason that unlawful activity were suspected.

While I support this law in it's protection of law-abiding citizens, I feel that the current interpretation of this law has become an unintended hindrance to stopping criminal activity. Often, the judge will disallow the use of incriminating evidence in court cases, based on some trumped up protest from a criminal lawyer.

The rule should be that if the evidence that has been found appears to indicate criminal activity, then it should be assumed that there was just cause to search for it. This does not mean that law enforcement should be allowed to do anything that they are not allowed to do presently, but any evidence that is incriminating should be usable against the criminal. If the law enforcement personnel has violated the Fourth Amendment, then the law enforcement person should be held accountable. But again, if the evidence is incriminating, it should be useable against the person. In other words, if the person is a criminal, they need to be treated as such. An irregularity in how we found that out should not change the fact that they are a criminal.

In determining if the enforcement person were guilty of violating the Fourth Amendment, it should require a judge or jury to determine that guilt. If "hot pursuit" were involved, that should be taken into account. If time allowed, then the more rigorous processing of a warrant should be required. But if incriminating evidence were found, the courts should be very careful to give the benefit of the doubt to the enforcement personnel. Remember that they are acting in behalf of the safety of the population when in pursuit of criminals or criminal activity. Often they must make split second decisions. They constantly risk their safety (and in this case freedom) for the public safety. The law was originally intended to preclude planned violations of privacy, not incidental activity while in hot pursuit. And it certainly was not intended to protect a criminal.

GHETTOES

Starting at a very early age, we begin to be influenced by our social environment. While we are always driven by our own psyche, we form opinions, develop philosophies and establish goals, based in a large part on what we observe around us. The material success or failure of those around us influences us, as well as the social esteem or disgust that is applied to those individuals by others in the community. Often, a young person will follow a way of life similar to their families or others who live in their area because they gradually become involved in their activities.

Fortunately, we all rethink our opinions, philosophies, and goals several times during our process of maturing. This process of maturing actually continues throughout life. People see things differently at many times throughout their lives. Some of us remember when the "Beatniks" used to say "You cannot trust anyone over 35". What that was all about is the fact that the Beatniks were idealistic (or optimistic, depending on your age) about changes to social customs, while the more mature people would stifle their ideas. But the point it makes is that our thinking changes throughout out lives.

If the society we observe around us does not change, we may have a narrow field from which to choose our goals. In a ghetto area, we do not see the best examples of social or moral behavior. Because of the lack of good examples, and also the lack of opportunities, it is hard to rise above the culture and economic capacity of the ghetto.

We need some way to assist the people of the depraved areas in seeing the advantages of rising above the way of life that pervades their area. They need to be exposed to enough new ideas, and get enough encouragement, so that their opinions, philosophies and goals rise above those of the existing ghetto areas. We must find a way to get those ideas to them and help them develop higher goals and give them hope in their ability to achieve them. Then we must give them the initiative to follow them.

Sometimes, the simplest and most obvious way of doing things is the best, but sometimes we overlook the obvious things. With that in mind, let me suggest a series of billboard messages placed in such a way that nearly everyone in the ghetto area cannot help but read the message. Or better yet, lets pass out some papers, door to door, on a weekly or monthly schedule, with helpful messages.

It is important that the messages be simple and short so that they are taken in at a glance. I believe that they will work their way into the thinking of the ghetto population. It does not matter if they miss some occupants or if they are laughed at by everyone. Even if they are made fun of, they will at least provoke thought and maybe influence the ideas, philosophies and goals of some people. It should at least suggest that there is a better way of life, and that they can achieve it. Clear instructions are needed in order to get them started.

Let me suggest some messages:

First, for the billboard:

1. There is a better way to live.
2. To get a job, you must speak clearly. Work on that.
3. Dress neatly for job interviews, no baggy pants.
4. You can do it.
5. Take responsibility for your own life.
6. Do something good.

7. Don't have sex if the child will live <u>here</u>.

8. Drugs = very short feel good.

   Drugs = very long feel bad.

9. Sex without marriage = worthless fathers.

Next, for the papers:

1. There is a better way to live.

   You can do it.

   Take responsibility for your own life.

   If your friends are holding you back, get away from them.

2. The first step in getting away from this area is to get a job. You can learn a skill by getting a job.

   To get a job, you must be able to speak clearly. If people are asking you to repeat things, or do not know what you are saying, you must improve your speaking before you will be able to get a job. Nearly all jobs require you to talk to people. You will not be hired unless people can understand you.

Go to _____ (State Board of ...) located at _____ to get help in finding a job.

Be sure to dress neatly, no baggy pants.

3. Having sexual activity without marriage may cause another child to live in this poverty. Do not do this to them.

4. Encourage the children in the area to go to school and try to do well. The better they do in school, and the farther they go in school, the better the chances they have of having a better life after they finish school.

5. Drugs = very short feel good.

   Drugs = very long feel bad.

6. Try to be the "good person" in your neighborhood. It is a good feeling, and good practice for when you get to a better neighborhood.

7. No one will improve your life for you. You must do it yourself. But you <u>can</u> do it yourself. Get started now.

8. If you have children, it is up to you to do things to help them have a better life. Encourage them in school. Get them to a better neighborhood.

Always know whom they are with.

9. The better you speak, and the better you dress, the better the job you can get.

10. Talk to a Priest or Minister for advice in all things. They can help.

Exercise

Exercise is very important to our health. In bygone times, we got plenty of exercise in the course of earning a living, doing domestic chores, and getting around. Now, most of us need some artificial way of tuning up our cardiovascular system, developing our muscular system, and controlling our weight. As we get older, exercise takes on an additional meaning: - <u>Use it or lose it!</u>

But exercise is similar to going to Church. Either we go on a regular schedule, without exception, or we go only on Christmas and Easter. There is always a reason (EXCUSE!) for skipping a session – too tired, too busy, something hurts, there is something else that we want to do at that time… Somehow, many of us never get around to setting up the routine. Our only exercise may come at a couple of family picnics in the summer.

Let me give you a tip on how to make it easier to get into the routine. Find something that you like to do, and make it your activity. Become a fanatic about doing it at a regular time (and frequently). Be aggressive about picking something that will extend your physical capacity. Some examples that I have seen are: walking, running, bowling, tennis, swimming, table tennis, volleyball, and basketball. I have even seen people around 80 years old, playing a game called chair volleyball, in a league. In chair volleyball, which is played on a smaller court, six people on each side hit a beach ball back and forth while they must remain in their seat.

Excuse me for insulting your intelligence, but because of some quirks in our legal system, I must warn you to consult your doctor before you try anything mentioned in this essay. I do not want to be sued for failing to tell you that.

If you pick an activity, such as walking, that does not require your mental attention, you can reduce the mental boredom and the awareness of tiredness by listening to a radio. If you are using a stationary exercise machine, you can even watch television. It is important to get your mind off of the fact that your body is tired, or the workout will be short.

I recommend something competitive, if you are up to it. That will take your mind off the tiredness, and push you to work to meet the challenge. Your competitive spirit will bring out the adrenalin to overcome the fatigue. But you may have to accept the risk of injury. Competition implies that you are not in complete control.

Let me give as an example, a group of senior citizens who have found that it is easy to be active if you enjoy what you are doing. This is a group that plays basketball every Tuesday, Thursday, and Saturday at 9:00 in the morning. They play half court games for at least and hour and a quarter, and sometimes longer. The group includes anyone who is 50 years old or over, but there are very few under 60, except on Saturday. You would be surprised and impressed by the quality and intensity of the games.

Let's move ahead to where you have chosen an activity and found a way to get started doing it on a regular basis. Then one time you are a little tired and are considering skipping it just once. Before you let the "only Christmas and Easter" syndrome set in, think of the following true story.

Don Baker was one of those senior citizens involved in the over 50 basketball group mentioned above. Don was an average player. He could make a shot if he could get open, and worked hard on defense.

Don was very service oriented and was always helping someone. One day, while he was mowing a field for a friend, his tractor threw him off, and the bush cutter he was pulling caught him. Don lost his right arm at the shoulder, and had serious damage to the muscle and flesh at his hip. Don spent some time in the hospital, and was fitted with a short prosthetic arm.

In a few months, Don started coming again to the basketball sessions. He spent about six weeks, by himself at one of the unused baskets, trying to learn how to shoot left-handed. That is not as easy as you might think. Not only do you have to learn how to use the left hand, but you must do it without the help of the other hand. The footwork is also different.

Now Don plays in the games whenever he is needed to make an even number of players. His offense is not so great. But he plays good defense and rebounds. Any coach will tell you that footwork is the most important part of those skills. Don also continues to be an active member of the Volunteer Fire Department. Oh, did I mention that Don is 70 years old!

The next time you are tempted to skip an exercise session, remember Don Baker and judge your excuse accordingly.

REGRETS

I do learn. Sometimes I am a bit slow to learn, but I do learn. For example, just three weeks ago was the first time in my life that I pulled my hand back when someone deflected a pass that was thrown to me in a basketball game. My usual reaction is for my hand to follow the ball after the deflection, and the result is usually that I am the last one to touch the ball before it goes out of bounds. Today, I again pulled my hand back and my team got the ball. So, you see, I have learned. But, at age 68, I must admit that I was slow to learn.

Now, this slow-to-learn problem occurred once before in my life. Back in college, it was my senior year. I had done fairly well in my technical classes up to that point, and was looking forward to graduating with a degree in Engineering. But in each test that I took in a class entitled "World Literature", I received a grade of "55". Nothing was marked incorrect, just the grade of 55 was written on the exam booklet. I never seemed to learn that the grade was based on length. I just answered the questions as concisely as I could, - as we were taught to do in the engineering classes.

I should have figured it out, because one of my classmates received a grade above 90 on one of the tests, but he had answered all five questions incorrectly. His answers all described the wrong monster guarding the River Styx in "Dante's Inferno". But he did write long answers.

I hate to admit it, but I got an "F" in that subject in two straight report periods. I was suspended. Now, lest you think that I am an "engineering geek", and cannot do anything but math, I must tell you that I received an award from the State of Ohio for English when I was in high school.

But now let me show you that I did learn about writing at length. Upon my return to school, I was required to take a course in "Western Civilization". On the first quiz, which was an essay about the battle of Thermopylae, I filled up one side of a paper with many lines, very close together and quite small handwriting. The teacher handed the quizzes back to the 80 students in decreasing order of grades. My grade was a "78". It was somewhere around the middle. The teacher had let graduate students check the quizzes. The only red marks on my quiz were question marks after the names of two of the lesser commanders, and at the top of the paper they had written: "This is an excellent essay".

A friend of mine received a grade of "92", which was the second highest of the 80 papers. It took much persuasion to get him to let me see his quiz. It covered four pages, but the paper was smaller, with the lines farther apart, and the writing was larger than mine. Furthermore, he had skipped every other line. The graduate student had made many red marks all over his paper. At the top of the first page was written: "This is B.S. not an essay."

Well, for the second quiz I acquired some grade school style paper with the lines far apart and big margins. I left additional margins, skipped lines, and filled up five pages. The question was "What is the Investiture Controversy?" The only thing that I knew was that it had something to do with the question of who appoints the Bishop in a country, the Pope or the King. (No, this was not a private school.) One whole page and half of another described a snowstorm in the mountains because the Pope has his winter quarters at Castel Gandalfo, which I think is in the mountains. Anyway, I got the second highest grade: 92. By the end of the year, I was exempt from the final exam because I had over a 90 average.

So you see, I did learn.

But doesn't this story upset you? Does it make you disrespect non-technical graduates? Does it make you wonder what we can do to check up on our colleges? The word "phony" pops into my mind.

But here is the worse part. Back then, I made a decision not to discuss this with (complain to) the College officials. I had worked so hard to get that far that I did not want to take any chances of having my college records spoiled. There have always been bad things happening to "whistle blowers". Furthermore, I felt that the school officials would just think that I was trying to get revenge for a bad grade. In other words, I did not feel that I would have credibility.

So here is the real problem. People are afraid to expose bad situations. Employers tend to find ways to get rid of "troublemakers". Once you have a reputation as a whistle blower, it is hard to find a job. Your whole life can be changed by one responsible action. (Yes, I said responsible.)

If a person reacts to save another person's life by putting his own life in danger, we treat him as a hero. Sometimes he is rewarded, either directly or indirectly, because of his heroic reputation. It is time that we start to consider whistle blowers as heroes. If enough of us start rewarding these good deeds, maybe the trend will catch on and people will be more willing to take the risk.

It really bothers me today, that I was unwilling to do something back then to discredit those teachers! Back then, my anger was toward those persons who were abusing their positions. Today, my regret is that I didn't try to fix the system by discussing the situation with the Department Heads, or higher.

Practical Education

There are a lot of reasons for having a public school system. Preparation for earning a living is a very important one, but it is not the only one.

I was once told that the purpose of an education is to enable me to get more out of life. In those days, an education was not as crucial in finding a job. It does emphasize that there is more than one reason to have a school system available to everyone. A broad education would be a help in developing a philosophy of life, and equally importantly, in understanding one's own situation. Often, we think of philosophy as a religious concept, and they certainly are related. But even the people who choose an atheistic philosophy usually seem to come up with a higher purpose. Typically, they develop a "duty to preserve nature" type of philosophy. In any case, the broader the education, the more fully one can understand the purpose of life and what is expected of them.

Another, and obviously very important, part of the education system is learning to get along with each other, and how to act in society. In this, the present system is failing. The cause of the failure is the legal system. The current laws make it very difficult to establish a meaningful disciplinary system. Even applying a properly administered disciplinary measure is risky because of the ability of parents, students, and lawyers to distort the truth. Winning a lawsuit can be tremendously profitable for parents and lawyers, and losing can be devastating to a teacher or administrator. Even a successful defense in a lawsuit can cost several years salary. Because of this, discipline has pretty much disappeared in the public school system, and to some extent in the private schools. Without the ability to enforce rules and a standard of conduct, there is no hope of teaching anything related to proper conduct or discipline or morals.

Students will always set their own standards of conduct based on peer pressure. If there are no enforceable rules of conduct imposed upon them, and no moral principles taught to them, then some of the students will be establishing a pretty nasty standard for the others to follow. Some will learn how easy it is to become bullies, and the advantage of being feared. In higher grades, this develops into formation of and joining into gangs. Use of tobacco, drugs, alcohol, and engaging in sex are always temptations, but when the only punishment for being caught is to be given a short vacation from school (suspension), the incentive to resist temptation is small.

Peer pressure is large. Furthermore, the effects are synergistic, which means that if some do it because they can do it, then others feel the need to do it too, in order to fit in. Pretty soon, nearly everybody adopts a lower standard of social behavior. It usually turns out that trying to be a good student is not a respectable behavior either. Also, remember that the kids are not only living by those standards while in school, but they are learning a way of life. Even if they practice a double life by being sweet little children at home, they may choose the lower standard for themselves later, when parents are not looking over their shoulder. In any case, the teaching of proper social behavior and self-discipline, and providing an incentive to learn, are all falling short because of the legal system.

Some would suggest that the basic life skills should be taught at home. I would agree, except that it isn't happening. It is very difficult for a mass education system to address this area because much of this is culturally diverse material. For example, absolutely everyone should know how to cook. But, not only would each ethnic background have a different approach to this, but every family unit would have different staple foods. In other words, they should learn how to cook, but not what to cook. Somehow, learning to satisfy a basic need seems more important than learning to calculate a square root.

There are other things that we need to know: How a checking system works, how to write the checks, and how to balance a checkbook. How credit and debit cards work and what are the costs of credit and the penalties for late payment. What is stock and how do you buy it. What are the tax requirements and how do you file a return. How do you properly fill out a job application or write a resume. I think it would help the average student more if they taught them how to purchase a home, than to teach them who shot Abe Lincoln. By the way, a good course in manners wouldn't hurt either.

OUR DEBT

From time to time, we hear a claim from people of African-American descent that our government (or society) owes them something because of their abuse in the past. There are also claims from Native-American Indians about our taking their land. Jewish people occasionally make claims about their losses during the Nazi regime.

Naturally, our reaction is to say that we do not owe them anything because we did not do anything ourselves to harm them. We feel sorry that those things happened, but we shouldn't have to give up anything we have because of something someone else did to them in the past.

Now there are three angles from which to view their situation: economic, legal, and ethical. (Not to mention the psychological categorization as "crybaby".)

From the economic point of view, these situations of the past surely did have an effect on the current situation. Of course, it would be extremely difficult to pin down any individual cause and effect, and that would be necessary for any claim to be valid. For example, you could say that slavery has caused the black population to be some percentage less well off financially than the white population of the United States. But you could also say that the black population of the United States is some percentage better off financially than the black population of some specific African country. No specific individual African-American can be fairly identified with either of these situations. I don't owe them anything as a result of their slavery of 150 years ago, and they don't owe me anything for bringing them to the relative prosperity of being in the United States, as opposed to a less prosperous African country, and for freeing them from slavery in the Civil War. I realize that de facto segregation continued long after the Civil War, but from the economic aspect of it, not everyone has the same opportunities in any civilization.

In other words, yes, past situations have had an economic effect on everyone. But in our society, everyone has a different economic heritage. We can only hope to be fair to everyone as we move on from where we are now. By now, although significant familial inheritance surely gives an advantage, pretty much everyone has the opportunity to earn a decent living.

From the legal point of view, the overriding principle is the Statute of Limitations. For an individual case, you need the courts to decide. But whether the Statute applies as written or not, the fact that our forefathers saw the need for that type of limitation speaks strongly for the need to accept things as they are, and move on. For example, think of how much better off the Palestinians would be if they had ignored Israel by about 1960 and began to live their own lives. They could have avoided two generations of poverty, killing, being killed and having only hatred and despair for a way of life. But instead, they concentrated on wanting to regain some land that they lost, and would not move on.

Now the American Indian situation needs some additional comments, although the Limitation principle still applies. First of all, their culture did not define individual ownership. Hunting grounds, for example, were for common use. In addition, many of the tribes were nomadic and therefore did not even establish "squatter rights". While it is true that they were here first, they did not establish a system of ownership or control that was compatible with the larger population that was developing. The new population simply overwhelmed them and established their own law of the land and rules of ownership. Certainly, the original inhabitants should be allowed equal rights and ownership of any property they already occupied. But compensation at this late date should be precluded by the Statute of Limitations, unless there were documented agreements regarding something. Of course, any previous agreements should be honored.

In other words, from both the legal and the economic points of view, the claims are obsolete. Move on!

Now, from the ethical or moral point of view, we need to be sure that all people have opportunity for life, liberty, and the pursuit of happiness. We need to be sure that no one is deprived of these opportunities, and that those people who need help in that regard are given that help. Of course, portions of those rights can be forfeited by the individual's behavior, such as criminal activity or psychological, emotional or mental disorders that make them a danger to other people.

From the moral aspect, it is not enough to say that no one is being deprived of those opportunities. In many cases, they may need assistance. We tend to give welfare payments, and free services, but we need to "teach them to fish" as the story goes. Naturally, we must continue to provide temporary aid to those needing it, and permanent aid to those needing it. But we must be proactive in developing progress with anyone who is disadvantaged. It doesn't matter if we feel that all black residents of the ghetto have had several generations to rise above poverty or not, we need to actively assist them, both as individuals and as an element of society, in developing the skills, attitude, confidence and social skills that will help them achieve a respectable level of existence. We must recognize that, with some exceptions, they have the mental and physical potential to rise to a respectable level. They may need assistance in learning how to get there.

Government can and should make assistance and training available. Charitable agencies can and should provide for material needs, but must also work on training and attitude adjustment. Employers should provide apprenticeships and training. But individuals must treat the disadvantaged with respect, compassion and charity.

Somehow, through all these sources, we must get to each disadvantaged individual and help them learn what they need to know and give them the confidence and motivation to progress. Then, and only then, will we be free of our debt to the past.

Penance

Years ago, the Church imposed much physical penance on its people. There were clearly defined rules for fasting during Lent. Even if you were not required to fast, by age or disability or if you did strenuous work, you were expected to "give up" something for Lent. All year long, no one over seven years of age was allowed to eat meat on Friday. In Confession, penances were given. Long ago, a penitent might be required to wear a rough feeling garment, or he might be required to work among the disadvantaged. Sometimes, he would be required to stand in a public place, dressed in sackcloth, and beg passers by to pray for him.

Did the physical penance do us any good in helping to erase any responsibility before God for our bad actions? I am sure it helps. But that was not the only important part of the penance philosophy. Consider the following (partial list, I am sure):

1. Performing a physical act makes a far greater impression on the psyche than merely hearing or reading about something. Therefore, the

more penance we do, the more conscious we become of the need to avoid doing bad things.

2. The more time we spend doing things that call our attention to our relation to God, the more we become aware of our relation to God. It really helps if we are aware of some responsibility other than to satisfy our inclination to please ourselves.

3. It reminds us that actions have consequences, and bad actions have bad consequences, and those consequences hurt. We are smart enough to conclude that means either now or later.

4. Making ourselves do anything, whether it is our idea or some Church official's, is a part of developing a self-discipline.

5. The community awareness of our religious activities, such as fasting, is good because of the synergism it develops within our own religion. It can also at least start a dialogue with outsiders.

But self-discipline is of special importance today. Young people today do not have a rigorous self-discipline. They are not trained in self-discipline in the school systems. School administrators fear legal action if they do anything related to discipline. Parents do not provide the training at home. In many families, the parents are not at home with the children all the time, or even enough time to impose the disciplined life style that is important to have in order to react properly to the situations that present themselves to each of us. Children are brought up in a culture that emphasizes personal freedoms as opposed to moral correctness and the self-discipline that is required to make the correct choices. We are certainly no longer a tough, morally correct society.

Natural Fathers

Much has been said about the public school system in regard to the difference between schools in ghetto areas and schools in suburban areas. The difference in test scores is given as proof of inferiority of the schools.

Now many people will claim this is because there is a difference in intelligence between the races. Others claim the school board takes better care of the suburban area schools. Others claim that testing is directed at things that are related to ethnic culture and history.

I want to call for a study that shows whether there is any relationship between test scores and whether or not the students are being raised by their natural fathers. I suspect this may be the real controlling factor.

Don't get me wrong. I am not claiming that ghetto dwellers are more prone to sex outside marriage than others. I am only suggesting that when men do not remain with their offspring, they not only put the offspring at a financial disadvantage which forces them to live in a blighted area, but they also put them at a cultural disadvantage. Without a good role model, the children may not be encouraged to attend school regularly and to apply themselves sufficiently to achieve an education.

There may be just as much illicit sex in wealthier areas, but the effect is not as devastating because there may be sufficient financial resources to get around the problems that are overwhelming in the financially disadvantaged areas.

Some major school board may be able to do this study as part of their normal operation, but I hope that they also query other school boards in order to get an answer that includes diversity. If schools (who may already have this information at their disposal) cannot do this study, then perhaps some graduate student can make this study into a thesis.

Of course, once we know if this is the problem, then we need to do something about it. I have ideas about that, but I need the studies in order to motivate people to solve the problem.

LAWS

Our country is controlled largely by our legal system. That is very good. It lessens the probability that people will be treated unfairly or unequally. It sets a standard that, if followed rigorously, will define our level of safety, freedom, individuality, economic opportunities, etc. This is defined in the Constitution as establishing justice and ensuring domestic tranquility.

Of course, there can be weaknesses. If it is not applied equally, the entire concept crashes. In many countries, a dictator or ruling class or whatever, takes control of the system and it is too bad for the outsiders. Perhaps the genius of our country's legal system is the counterbalancing of power by establishment of the three branches of government: Legislative, Executive, and Judicial. The fact that each of the 50 states has a hand in determining who operates each branch is a major equalizing factor. This makes it very difficult for a strong and ruthless group from one area to get control over the whole system. There are too many diverse and widely separated individuals who would have to be won over for a power play to work.

Even with these controls though, there can be unfair application of the law at a local level, or in isolated areas. A perfect example of the local level case would be the prejudicial treatment of blacks in the south after the civil war and on into the 1960's. I am not referring to laws that discriminated, because they were often consistent with the Constitutional definition of blacks at that time. I am referring to situations similar to the book/movie "To Kill a Mockingbird", where an innocent black man was unfairly convicted and then murdered in order to protect a guilty white man. A deterrent to this is the freedom of the press and the "Freedom of Information Act". It is still not perfect, but new laws forbid discrimination due to a variety of things: race, color, religion, sex, national origin, handicap, ancestry, or age. (My niece pointed out to me that Attitude is not on the list.)

The flexibility to change the laws, and even the Constitution itself is very important. It is good, however, that it is very difficult to change the Constitution. Personal interest groups have a way of concentrating their power in a way that is far out of proportion to their constituency. If we change the Constitution, we need to be sure that the change is important, fair, and has a reasonable expectation of permanency.

Sometimes laws outlive their usefulness. An example of this would be the subsidies and protections enacted for tobacco farmers. For some reason, these laws are still in effect, even though the overwhelming majority wishes that tobacco users were non-existent.

Sometimes laws are written for good reasons, but the resultant use of them is counterproductive. An example of this is the set of laws that protects us from false accusations and defamation of character. As a result of the lawsuits developing from these laws, and the associated costs, it has become common practice to only give the starting and ending dates of employment when a previous employer is called for reference. Most companies will not share information with the person who was referred to them. They will not say whether the person quit or was fired, or anything else that could be relevant. The example of this that comes to mind involves a long-term care facility that found that one of their employees had killed several patients. During investigation, it was learned that the employee had been "let go" by another hospital under suspicion that he had killed some of their patients. If I remember correctly, the first hospital had actually been contacted as reference in this case, but even if they had not been contacted, it would have been because it is known that it is a waste of time to ask. Fear of lawsuits has broken down the referencing system.

For many reasons, it is important that our laws, at least below the Constitution level, be regularly examined and evaluated. Today, our laws are scattered into many groupings. It is good that laws exist on the local, state, and national levels. But with the many different enactments at each of those levels, spread over so many years, and the inclusion of many related and unrelated topics into each act, it is impossible for one person to be aware of everything they need to know about the law.

We need to develop a Codification, with cross-references where needed, so that we can reasonably easily find all we need to know about a subject, find duplications and contradictions, simplify the language, and most of all, be able to evaluate the overall effectiveness of the law. I firmly believe that this reevaluation needs to have more than just lawyers working on it. I think that it is all but impossible to get a broad grasp of the laws without a good system of bringing all the laws together that are involved in any topic.

MIDDLE EAST

A deliberately provocative set of political cartoons was published in a Danish newspaper. They were aimed at the Islamic population. Although they were not published in the United States, I understand that they included depictions of Mohammed, including one with a bomb for a headdress, referring to terrorist activity in his name.

There were riots by the Islamic populations of many countries. The Islamic religion forbids images of Mohammed and other religious persons.

We could talk about freedom of the press or about the rights of free speech. The press has already addressed those points because they are crucial for them.

We could analyze the religious basis for the riots. As I understand it, it is based on a tradition that was developed as an attempt to prevent an image from becoming an object of idolatry. I don't think there is any danger of these particular images becoming an object of idolatry.

But those academic arguments miss the big picture. If those Islamic followers, who rioted in defense of some aspect of their religion, did nothing when some Islamic people killed people in the name of the Islamic religion, then they may have approved of that action. If they feel obligated to point out one thing that is objectionable by their religion, why do they not try to demonstrate their objection to or disassociation with an Islamic group who plants bombs in various civilian areas and infers that God (Allah) wants them to do it. I have to conclude that they are not appalled that someone would kill people and use Islam as their excuse.

On the other hand, I wonder if they are afraid to say anything against certain segments of their "civilization" for fear of reprisal. Let's face it, the people to whom they would be giving trouble, are prone to violence. This sounds like it may be a classic case of bullying. It seems like, especially in Iraq, the faction with the most weapons controls the lives of the weaker. It is ironic that in the precise area that was considered the "cradle of civilization" they haven't progressed past rule by bullying.

Further evidence that this is a big part of the problem is that Iraq and Iran fought for something like seven years. Supposedly, it had something to do with the fact that Iran was controlled by the Shiite sect and Iraq was controlled by the Sunni sect, both of which are Islamic. Iraq has been accused of mass exterminations using chemical weapons as part of that war. They are also accused of mass exterminations with the Kurdish population of their own country. If you add this to the fact that Iraq, at the time of the war and the exterminations, was controlled by a minority group, the Sunnis, and that they had a reputation for intimidation and torturing their own subjects, you get the impression that the most savage group rules. They don't seem to mind using weapons on anyone who opposes them. It is a true terrorism controlled civilization. A similar situation seems to accompany the Taliban in Afghanistan.

Now that the former regime (Sunni) has been unseated, and a new government has been democratically elected, you would expect more stability. But the group that had the upper hand before still has weapons and still has an inclination to use them. At first, their aim was at the peacekeeping force (from our point of view … occupation force from their point of view) and the new government's police force. Later, they have begun terrorist activity against the Shiites directly. They have even blown up the Shiite's most sacred Mosque, as well as exploded bombs at Shiite gatherings.

If they get their way as a result of these terrorist actions, it would be a shame. But it has worked in the past! I wonder how many of them would remain devoted to their particular sect if they did not have to fear for their lives if they showed some disloyalty.

Another incident of the bullying is the pressure applied by the local rulers in the case of the Afghani who was seen with a Bible. When they learned that he was a convert to Christianity, they brought charges against him and were seeking the death penalty. As a result of international pressure, they agreed that he would not have to stand trial, because of insanity, but he was deported. He now lives in another country and is said to fear for his life. Need I say more?

Unwed Mothers

Allow me to use the phrase "unwed mothers" to mean that they were unwed at the time of conception and remained unwed. Statistics show that the children of these unwed mothers do not do well in life.

I see figures like 70 percent of the juveniles in state reform institutions come from fatherless homes. There are several sources that claim that the relationship between single parent families and crime is stronger than the relationships between poverty and crime or between race and crime. A bad start of this type is going to be difficult to turn around in later life.

This puts a great drain on society. There is much welfare money (yours and mine taxes) spent on both the children and the unwed mother. Also, their excessive contribution to the criminal element makes our life much more uncomfortable and costs us even more money in terms of insurance and even more taxes to support additional law enforcement. Increased taxes and insurance are also paid by businesses as a result of the larger criminal element, which makes their products go up in price, and we have to again pay more because of these children.

There is no way society can prevent this from happening once to each unwed mother, except maybe parental love and attention coupled with general education and specific education about morals, sex, economics, discipline, etc. But those approaches take several generations to establish and decadence seems to trump progress in those areas.

It seems, however, that women who have one illegitimate child often have more. I know one woman who has just had her fourth and has never been married. And, she certainly has figured out many ways to get society (you and me) to pay her way. So since we cannot stop the first one, lets look at how we can stop the rest.

There are many extreme measures that could be tried, but none that are acceptable. Neutering is a form of mutilation and is considered immoral by many, and I agree. Similarly, the death penalty is out of the question. Abortion snuffs out a human life, and an innocent one at that. I wonder what happens to the human soul of someone who does not live long enough to please God, as is the case when an abortion occurs. Confinement is an interesting idea, either in prison or in an isolated communal society. I know this could never happen, because Americans emphasize individual rights, but it is interesting to think about.

So that leaves us with maybe trying to find a way to support the children. Some women will want to keep the child and some will want to put the child up for adoption. Adoption may be good, if the natural mother and father are of the type who would not make good parents. With a good promotional program, we may be able to place more children than we do now. But even there, the natural parents should be made to contribute something to cover the expenses.

Now we are at the crux of the matter. We need to make the natural parents carry more of the financial (and maybe parenting) burden associated with these children. They have a moral obligation to do this anyway, and if they cannot get out of it, that may serve as a deterrent. But the current laws are the problem. If the courts determine that the father owes child support, it is only enforceable in the state where the court action is initiated. Often fathers just move to another state and another court action is required. The cost of this court involvement is often prohibitive even in the first state, but it is absurd to have to repeat this action. <u>We need to have court action initiated automatically by the local government and enforceable in any state.</u>

In addition to the need to have the support mandate enforceable nationally, we need to make the process of identifying the natural father into a thorough and practical process. The mother should be required to identify the father or potential fathers. Failure to do so should bring serious penalties. Mandatory DNA testing should be required for anyone so identified. Once the father is thereby identified, he should be required to provide support until the child is fully grown and educated. In the case of adoption, both the natural mother and natural father should be required to contribute in some manner, either a stipend or an ongoing contribution through an agency.

If you want this to happen, write your Congressman, both for the national rule and for the DNA stipulation. You can help it happen!

Let this be a challenge for someone to find a way to make out of wedlock pregnancies illegal, with penalties and financial obligations for both the parents. I would not be opposed to removing the child from the natural parents, at least until they can demonstrate that they are ready to take care of them physically, mentally and emotionally. If they are single, it may be because they were not yet ready for the task, either economically or emotionally. They may not be capable of earning sustenance for either themselves or the child. It may be even worse if they do find work and let the child or teenager to raise themselves. Ultimately, that could cost society even more. This out-of-wedlock phenomenon may be the largest reason why ghettoes sprawl and never go away. If we can spend some tax money at this crucial time, and squeeze some money out of each natural parent, and maybe get a little volunteer participation, maybe we could end the "vicious cycle" that goes with the inadequate rearing of children by unwed mothers.

The out of wedlock phenomenon is not confined to the ghetto. It is just easier to find a supporting adult in places where economic conditions are better. Someone other than the natural parents is still going to be burdened. It can still provide problems for society by disrupting the existing families, especially if one or more of the parents are married to someone else.

Nuclear Power

A decade or two ago, the utility industry in the United States opted to stop building nuclear power plants. It was costing too much to keep re-engineering and retrofitting the unfinished plants to keep up with the changes that the government kept making in the regulations.

I was part of the effort to build one of the nuclear plants. It was close to completion several times. Finally, after too many changes and setbacks, it was converted to a coal burning power plant and put on line as such.

There were over 100 nuclear plants completed and put into operation before America gave up on construction. In fact, in 2006, about 19% of the electricity produced in the United States was from 104 nuclear power plants. In the whole world, nearly 400 nuclear plants produced about 15% of the electricity.

Initially, the movement to nuclear power was supported by environmentalists. The mining of coal is a very dangerous operation. Not only is there very serious danger while digging, but the lung problem that coal miners face is very serious. Of course, the air quality is also affected by the combustion of coal.

But of course fear of the unknown is always a problem. Very few people understood the process. Many associated nuclear power with the atom bomb. Opponents played on the fears.

There were two incidents that occurred that helped build the case against nuclear power plants. In one of them, at Three Mile Island near Pittsburgh, there was an incident that received much publicity and caused much public reaction. No one was killed, and if someone had been standing against the perimeter fence during the entire incident, they would only have received about as much radiation as if they had received a chest x-ray.

The second incident was very serious. It occurred at Chernobyl in Russia. It devastated a very large area and killed or maimed a very large number of people. What is important to know, is that the Russian power plants at Chernobyl were fueled using a "graphite pile", which is the type used to produce fuel for atomic bombs.

Other than the "graphite pile" incident, I am not aware of any serious incidents. There is no comparison between regular nuclear power plants and "graphite pile" plants.

We need more nuclear power plants today for many reasons:

> To reduce the physical dangers, such as cave-ins, associated with working in underground mines.

> To reduce the health problems, such as black lung disease, faced by miners.

> To reduce atmospheric pollution from the combustion process of both coal and oil.

> To slow down the depletion of our coal and oil resources, which are useful for other purposes.

> To reduce the dependency on foreign oil which puts our economy in partial control of others.

> To reduce the potential for international crisis associated with the dependency on others for the supply of a critical material.

Let me remind everyone of a little history. The Japanese attack on Pearl Harbor, which brought us into World War II, was part of their effort to regain the oil supply, which had been closed to them. They thought that if they could disable our fleet they would be able to capture the sources of their lost oil supply. They did capture them, but did not count on our willingness to continue the war long enough to crush them. A lot of lives were lost in the four-year struggle.

THE REFORMATION

In the last few years, there have been numerous reported cases of priests being involved in sexual activity with minors. I suspect that this has always been happening with a small percentage of the priests. Psychologists will tell us that most victims will not report the incident or make it public for personal reasons. The fact that someone did report it, and the newspaper picked up on it, helped bring about an avalanche of similar reports. The fact that most of the incidents occurred many years before they were reported shows that there is truth in the theory that most victims are reluctant to talk about it. It also probably means that it has happened many times before the current rash of reports have surfaced. We probably just did not hear of them for reasons cited above.

By the way, this proves the theory that I have preached to my children. I have always claimed that it is easy to do bad things, like even robbing a bank and getting away with it. But for some reason, about one in ten times something goes wrong, like the getaway car gets a flat tire, or an off duty policeman is waiting in line to do some banking, or something. I always pointed out that when it does go wrong, the bad things that result from being caught make all the pleasant things seem trivial by comparison. This thing with the priests certainly proves the point that sooner or later, something will go wrong.

Although it is too early to have statistics, I expect that one result of this scandal is that many Catholics, and maybe even religious people in general, will become less attached to their religion. They may feel that the leaders (priests) are hypocritical and/or phony. They may even be embarrassed to belong to an organization that is associated with that sort of activity.

I can just imagine that this is the same sort of feeling that led to the Reformation. The Clergy were taking advantage of the generosity of the faithful and using the Church's resources to live excessively comfortable lives. They were perceived to drink excessively and live high. (I keep thinking of Friar Tuck from the Robin Hood movie.) Humans being what they are, there probably were occurrences of the same type of thing we are seeing today about sexual improprieties. To top it off, the special favors shown to the rich, and above all, the granting of indulgences (in reparation for sins) through generous alms, caused an urge for things to change.

The improvements in communication that were occurring at that time helped to spread the stories and helped to generate widespread opinions. All this led to lack of respect for the Clergy and also distrust of authority. The result was the breaking away from the long established Church and the establishment of new religious leaders. Of course, these also have splintered over the years, so that we now have a variety of religious sects.

Now the lessons to be learned from all this is that first, things that we do because we think no one will know that we did them and therefore we can get away with them, will backfire on us and cause us more grief than they are worth. And second, the more authoritative our position is, the more we must lead exemplary lives, because we are not only responsible for our own lives, but are also responsible for the image of the position we hold and the organization which we represent. I would not want to answer to God for being the cause of anyone, let alone millions of people, losing the benefit of a Church that He established for us.

What can you do about it? . . . Nothing, it is water over the dam. But examine your own life. If there is something you would not want someone else to know you did, don't do it!

Profits

Profits are essential to a capitalistic economic system. In general, the profit motive is what drives a person to establish a business that supplies a service, or produces, transports, or markets a product. These products and service are what raise our standard of living. They are the goods and services that make our lives easier and more enjoyable. The businesses also provide jobs for the majority of the people. Even if most of the people are not owners of a business, they owe their livelihood (earning power) to the fact that someone was motivated to form and operate a business.

Generally, prices and the resulting profitability are controlled inherently by such factors as the law of supply and demand, competition or the threat of it, perceived social needs of the local society, the affluence of the target market, the availability of alternates, etc. In the cases where abused could occur, such as the development of monopolies, the government can and should step in and regulate the operations, as they have done.

The government also needs to regulate the operations and charges by utilities. This is only partly because of the importance of these to normal urban life. It is also needed to insure that the utility companies provide adequate safety and adequate availability and quality of service. It is also because utilities normally are granted a franchise (monopoly) in order to prevent several electric pole lines or several gas lines from being built along the same street.

But, when it comes to pharmaceuticals, we had better let them make huge profits. There are two reasons for this. First, the research needed to develop new cures is extremely expensive. Also, there is a high risk that the research may be in vain. The cure may not be found. A very large profit potential is needed to encourage the research. Second, even though the research is very thorough (I hope), and all side effects are known and disclosed, there is always the chance that something will develop later, in accordance with Murphy's Law, that results in an expensive lawsuit.

I urgently need for them to continue to search for new and better ways to deal with medical problems. Let them make a profit!

Extramarital Sex

Sex outside of marriage is always a bad idea. There are obvious reasons for this and also some not so direct reasons. The obvious reasons include single women having to raise children. (See my essay on Unwed Mothers.) It also includes children being given up to orphanages. And, of course, there are the venereal diseases, including the newest one called AIDS. But there are some not so obvious situations that are more common than we would like to admit.

For example, if a married man has sex outside marriage, he will often get caught. (See my essay on not being worth it to do criminal activities.) This leads to divorce and often again to single women having to raise children.

Sometimes, when premarital sex leads to a pregnancy, the guy will be "honorable" and marry the girl after she becomes pregnant. While this is often a good thing to do, at least it may be the best thing to do at this stage of the situation, things will usually not be as good as they could have been if they had not had sex before marriage. Either or both parties may be forced to discontinue their education prematurely. There is a strong probability of causing reduced earning power. Their social status may be lessened, which again would lessen the chance that they may be offered more comfortable employment. The chances of divorce are high in the case where they got married only because of the pregnancy. Obviously, they may not be well suited for each other if they have only gotten together through a chance meeting ("got lucky"). But even if they were "going together", they may not have been together long enough to really know each other. Furthermore, if the time were right to be married, they would probably already be married. Therefore, getting married at that time is a risky marriage. Again, the chance is high for a single parent to be the result. The "right time" might not just be related to financial status or earning power. Many people are just not mature enough to handle marriage and children. Many still want to party irresponsibly or engage in "macho" activities such as drinking or fighting or whatever and lose their jobs and/or marriage because of it.

Even if no pregnancy is involved, word usually gets around about the situation. People like to brag. Word gets around fast. Once the "type of person" stigma is attached to a person, it may be hard to find a partner who can be depended on for proper support in marriage. But you can count on it being easier to find the wrong kind of partner if you have that reputation. Hence, it eventually leads to more unwed mothers and therefore, more poverty.

This is not to say that every single-parent situation is cause for embarrassment. Many single parents are the unfortunate result of an untimely death. Nor is the purpose of this essay to say that all single parents are in poverty. But it is quite difficult for a single parent to bring in a decent wage on a long-term basis, while maintaining control and providing for the physical, emotional and spiritual needs of one or more children.

THE TEST

I suspect our time on earth is both a punishment and a test. Now if it is a test, why are some tested more than others? I can't answer that about people who have a very short life span. But consider these ideas for the case where it looks easy for some and much harder for others. Take the case where a person is raised in a slum or ghetto versus a person raised in the wealthy part of town.

The ghetto provided plenty of temptation. Dope is available on every corner. Prostitution is visible. Gangs put a lot of pressure on people to join and then put a lot of pressure to commit crimes or beat up on people and whatever else. Gambling and drinking are pretty much a way of life. In addition to the temptation to partake of the available vices, there is the temptation to make a living (or at least earn some quick money) by providing those vices themselves.

But remember, the test is a spiritual test. It may be that the more affluent person is confronted by just as strong temptations. The subject matter may just be different, and may not be as visible to others. Maybe the affluent person knows someone who needs help, either financial or physical or spiritual, and fails to give it. Maybe someone is involved in certain types of businesses that do legal, but immoral things. I believe producing or selling cigarettes may fall into that category. Or maybe they operate a business that provides huge profits, but pays employees so little that they suffer greatly and have no stability or long term security. These may constitute a more serious offense than some of the vices practiced by those in the ghetto.

Many people walk around feeling superior because they do not partake of certain traditional vices such as those mentioned above. But their test might be on a different level. Maybe they have the capability to be a doctor but do not want to put in the effort to learn the profession, or they do not want the more rigorous lifestyle of a person responsible for the health of others. Or maybe they could be something else that would benefit others in society but instead they choose a more lucrative profession. These decisions and activities (or lack of) by the gifted or affluent people may affect many people. That seems a lot more serious than engaging in some of those vices in the ghetto, because it affects so many people.

Of course, wealthy people also have the same temptations as the others. There may be as much cheating on spouses and drunkenness and goofing off on the job among the affluent as with the poor people. I'll bet there is even more of the unsafe driving involved. Theft may take a different form, such as, cheating on taxes or insider stock transactions or whatever.

I haven't made you feel guilty, have I?

For Catholics Only

"You are Peter, and upon this rock I will build my church." Build indicates that He intended for it to be larger than just Peter. And, "Whatever you bind on earth shall be bound in heaven." These passages seem to indicate that it was Christ's intention to establish a church and also that he intended for it to be ongoing and authoritative.

In the Garden of Eden, man chose disobedience and tried to become like God, by obtaining the knowledge of good and evil. That can be considered both a sin of pride and of disobedience. So it makes sense that part of the punishment, or test, or whatever, on this earth would be the need to swallow the pride and let someone else be the authority requiring obedience and respect. At least for Christians, the Church that He established with Peter as the cornerstone would be that authority.

Even though we know that there is good and evil, sometimes we are confronted with things that blind us or confuse us, at least temporarily. If we simply allow the Church to be our authority, we can have no doubt that we are doing the right thing, because Jesus gave Peter that authority. See the first paragraph.

Often we are tempted to use "situation ethics" to make decisions. That means that we choose an option that seems like the best choice even though it is contrary to the teaching of the Church. But if we were capable of thinking it out thoroughly without our limited view and our prejudices, we might find that the Church was right. See the first paragraph.

An example of this is the practice of birth control. It is pretty easy to find worldly reasons not to have many children. Children use up the available family resources that are needed to provide a comfortable life for the other children (not to mention for one's self). Visions of not having such a nice house or car can be very blinding. But the Catholic Church (or more precisely, the Pope, who is the successor to Peter, and who can bind on earth) teaches that artificial birth control is wrong. (See the first paragraph.) So, let us explore some possible results if all Catholic families had about 12 kids, because they did not use artificial birth control or the alternative recommended by the church—natural family planning. This may help to show that there are often more significant results to each action than those that we may anticipate in our own little view.

While it seems pretty obvious that such a family would want even bigger housing, they might not be able to afford the upscale neighborhood. With less money available for housing after food and clothing, even allowing for the "Cheaper by the Dozen" factor, the large families might have to settle in the areas we now consider low class or even ghetto. Now at first, that seems to be a disaster. But if all Catholic families had about a dozen children, and maybe 80% of them would have to select low income housing, that would mean that about 20% of the entire U.S. population would be living in the low cost housing area simply because of their large family situation. That is in contrast to those living there because they are unable or unwilling to work for a decent living.

Now there are already many decent people living in that kind of area. There are many people who are low income because of a physical or mental handicap. There are also some who have suffered through some bad luck and do not have sufficient financial resources. There are even a very, very few people who take the Beatitudes seriously and live there for humanitarian purposes. But if you add the large Catholic (presumably well disciplined) families to the existing population of decent people, you just might have enough of a majority of decent people to create an atmosphere of decency. The synergism of that might allow almost all of the population in that area to prefer the decent life to the decadent life of crime and drugs now prevalent in the low cost housing areas. At least the children of the "other" element in the area would have more decent role models to follow.

Right now, the decent people may be a minority, and most probably are not the leadership types anyway. But synergism can be a strong force. Communication would surely accompany the large numbers. Generally, a community will respond to leadership of individuals and also will conform to the predominant culture of the members. Also, with the majority being good people, there is much more chance that people would have the courage to report crimes and thereby eliminate flagrant crime. While it is surely true that there are some people who are going to do the bad things that are now being done in these neighborhoods, it would be a little less comfortable for them. They are more likely to be turned in, and less likely to get off because no one will testify. They are not going to be the "respected" members of the community. And they will not be the only influence that the growing up generation will have, nor the only profitable way of life seen by the young people. Therefore, the entire culture of the ghetto area would improve morally. Maybe this is what God would expect of his people, instead of the selfish reasoning they are prone to follow, such as birth control.

Of course there are problems with this. The youth of the Catholic families will see some of the ways of life that are less moral than their parents would like them to see. But overall, the synergies would develop more good than harm. In any case, artificial birth control is not permitted by the Church, and we refer to the first paragraph above.

The ghetto example is not only just hypothetical, it is just not going to happen. But it does show that our narrow-minded decisions may differ from the rules laid down by an authority that was established by Christ. Maybe we should be following the higher authority. God's hope for us might not be served by taking pride in our ability to make our own decisions. Maybe by making our own decision, we are depriving the people of the ghetto areas of the chance they need to break out of their "vicious cycle" of bad examples, and to progress to a better life. Maybe we could provide a chance for them to be exposed to Catholicism. In any case, this example could demonstrate that we do not always know everything, and we need to always follow the authority of the Church. See the first paragraph.

Existentialism

Anyone who studies philosophy will know of the philosophy of "Existentialism". The short summary is that the only thing that matters in life is the memory of the person that is passed on after the person is dead. Now I am not recommending this philosophy as a religion, which it was. But I am pointing out that it might be a pretty nice thing if we can be remembered for something more than that we worked hard, enjoyed life, and raised a family.

With that in mind, I am suggesting that you pick a project that you think needs to be done, and get active in making it happen. Being remembered for your work, and maybe success, for some worthwhile project, is a nice thing to be hoped for. Perhaps you can look down from heaven and watch people giving you an award posthumously.

But some work provides reward even before death. My wife occasionally meets people that she worked with on one such project before she dropped out while she raised children. She can feel the mutual love and respect that these people have for each other. I also worked on several projects when I was young. I not only get a good feeling when I remember them, but a letter of recommendation from the project manager of one of them landed me a very good job. That job led to another very good job, which provided adequate funds to raise a family without my wife having to work. The job was enjoyable, provided opportunity for self-improvement and advancement, and allowed enough free time for me to be actively involved with my family. I have never met someone who was sorry they did "pro bono" work.

If you have a project in mind, go for it. The biggest need in the world is for someone to have a new idea and get it started. I hope that you can do that. But, if you cannot create a new idea, please pick one of the needs mentioned in this book of essays, and make it happen. Basically these are worldly needs that are waiting for someone to be the one who makes them happen. This is your chance to be remembered as the one who caused a good thing to happen. It is a level above just being one of the good people who helped with a project.

If you just get some project started, people will jump on the wagon and help. Most people are just waiting for someone to ask them to do something good, but very few people are self-starters. It takes someone to start the ball rolling.

Maybe this is a good time to summarize the needs that have been pointed out in these essays, so that you can pick a project.

Social: 1. We need to motivate and enable the ghetto dwellers.

2. We need to assure that all children receive support from both parents whether they are married or not.

Safety: 1. We need to make sure that threats to our safety (criminal acts) are minimized by making sure that incarceration is not being compromised by loopholes in the law or by lack of prisons.

2. We need to allow the appropriate agencies to do what they need to do to protect us from terrorism.

World: 1. We need to help the Middle Eastern countries understand that their refusal to accept Israel as a country is making their own lives miserable.

2. We need to make the world aware that public reaction to an image of Mohammad, coupled with their lack of public reaction to the killing of people in Allah's name, is an indication of a problem. That problem is that "tribal warfare" is their way of life in the Middle East, and that it is fueled by the religious leaders of the various sects. There needs to be a better system

of government in those areas that allows all people to have equal rights, regardless of their religious affiliation.

So there you are. Go ahead and start something that you will be remembered for. Existentially speaking, this is your big chance. Help me achieve my Existential goal by using this book as your incentive. As the TV commercials say: "Call now". In other words, get started right away. If you put it off, you will never do it.

About the Author

Jerry Eppy was the first from his family to go to college. His father offered to pay for his first year at college as an incentive to get him started, and also to let him live at home as long as he was in college. Jerry's family lived in a rented home in a working class neighborhood. By the time he was 21 years old, the demographics changed and it became an unsafe place to live. Even though he was a full time student, he used his savings to buy a house for himself and his parents in a safe neighborhood. He stepped up to the challenge/opportunity and purchased the house. He still managed to attain a Bachelor's Degree in Engineering, and a Master's Degree in Business Administration.

Jerry's career has been both varied and successful. He has been a machinist, a production foreman, and a plant engineer. He has worked for a public utility and managed a municipal electric and water utility. He has done sales work and customer-relations work. He has been in a Speakers Bureau and has spoken on topics such as Utility Financing, Energy Crisis, and Nuclear

Power. He has also found time to coach soccer, baseball, basketball, and track, all at the grade school level.

Jerry has raised his children to be involved in improving the quality of life for those around them. All of his children have done charitable work. One has a Master's Degree in Community Counseling, and has his name in the Governor's Hall of Fame for a program he wrote for use in the schools, regarding substance abuse. Another of his children has served in the Peace Corps.

Jerry Eppy is now begging others to step up and meet a need, as he did, and his children are doing, and not to offer excuses or look the other way. These essays are his attempt to promote awareness and maybe incite someone to action.

www.ingramcontent.com/pod-product-compliance
Lightning Source LLC
Chambersburg PA
CBHW020254290526
45784CB00003B/1241